2-14-82

GOOD MORNING, LORD

Prayers and Promises for Teens

Margaret Leonard Shiner

LIVING FAITH BOOKSTORE
8703 KANIS RD.
LITTLE ROCK, AR 72204
PH. 225-9678

BAKER BOOK HOUSE
Grand Rapids, Michigan

Copyright 1976 by
Baker Book House Company
ISBN: 0-8010-8079-7
Printed in the United States of America

First printing, December 1976
Second printing, September 1978
Third printing, October 1980

To
EARLE
who helped

1 HELP, LORD

"Open thou mine eyes, that I may behold wondrous things out of thy law" Ps. 119:18.

PRAYER:

Dear Lord, each year my problems grow
And I need answers daily.
Someone has said to search Your Word
To find the help I need.
I can't believe that You would care about my pesky, little trials
(They loom so large to me)
Or that Your Word of long ago
Would speak about my life today

But if it's so, I'm listening, Lord.

PROMISE:

"I, the Lord, will instruct you and teach you in the way you should go; I will counsel you with My eye upon you" Ps. 32:8, Amplified.

"The counsel of the Lord standeth for ever, the thoughts of his heart to all generations" Ps. 33:11.

"I am the Lord thy God, which brought thee out of the land of Egypt: open thy mouth wide, and I will fill it" Ps. 81:10.

"Let the word of Christ dwell in you richly in all wisdom" Col. 3:16a.

2 TEACH ME, LORD

"Lord, teach us to pray" Luke 11:1b.

PRAYER:

Dear Lord, help me to pray right.

Too long I've mumbled "God-bless" prayers and rattled on with stilted phrases.

Sometimes I tell my friends, "I'll pray for you," and then I fail to bring them and their needs before Your throne of grace.

At times I fail to ask for Your loving, healing touch when my own heart aches. I suffer needlessly.

And often when I kneel to pray, inwardly I'm standing, rushing to finish talking to you.

Oh, Lord, teach me to pray.

PROMISE:

"When thou prayest, enter into thy closet, and when thou hast shut thy door, pray to thy Father which is in secret; and thy Father which seeth in secret shall reward thee openly" Matt. 6:6.

"But when you are praying, first forgive anyone you are holding a grudge against, so that your Father in heaven will forgive you your sins too" Mark 11:25, TLB.

"Ask, and it shall be given you; seek, and ye shall find; knock, and it shall be opened unto you" Matt. 7:7.

3 ON OBEDIENCE

"Fear God, and keep his commandments: for this is the whole duty of man" Eccles. 12:13b.

PRAYER:

Dear Lord, I find it so hard to obey.
My parents say, "You must do...!"
Immediately I rebel—and not always inwardly.
My teachers lay down such strict rules
I find them hard to keep.
And everywhere I turn at work they tell me what to do....

Oh, God, I just remembered that Your Son was obedient unto death, even the death of the cross.

PROMISE:

"And Samuel said, Hath the Lord as great delight in burnt offerings and sacrifices, as in obeying the voice of the Lord? Behold, to obey is better than sacrifice, and to hearken than the fat of rams" I Sam. 15:22.

"Children, obey your parents in the Lord: for this is right" Eph. 6:1.

"Honour thy father and mother; which is the first commandment with promise; that it may be well with thee, and thou mayest live long on the earth" Eph. 6:2, 3.

"Remind your people to obey the government and its officers, and always to be obedient and ready for any honest work" Titus 3:1, TLB.

4 WITHOUT UPBRAIDING

"For the Lord is a God of knowledge" I Sam. 2:3b.

PRAYER:

Oh, Lord, it's testing time and I must be able to show all I have learned, but I am worried and afraid.

What if my mind goes blank?

I've studied hard and long, but possibly I've missed the point of some of the discussions.

My mind has wandered, too, at times, and I'll admit to some procrastination.

The possibility of low marks and failure haunts me. How I dread today's test!

I ask Your help. I seek Your wisdom, and I pray that You'll forgive me if I haven't studied as I should.

PROMISE:

"If any of you lack wisdom, let him ask of God, that giveth to all men liberally, and upbraideth not; and it shall be given him" James 1:5.

"A wise man will hear, and will increase learning; and a man of understanding shall attain unto wise counsels" Prov. 1:5.

"The fear of the Lord is the beginning of knowledge: but fools despise wisdom and instruction" Prov. 1:7.

"Happy is the man that findeth wisdom, and the man that getteth understanding" Prov. 3:13.

5 YIELD NOT

"Watch ye and pray, lest ye enter into temptation. The spirit truly is ready, but the flesh is weak" Mark 14:38.

PRAYER:

Oh, Lord, Temptation came to me, and I was severely tested.

He wore a cloak of gorgeous hue.

He sang praises to me until I shivered with delight.

He flattered me and made me feel so proud and exalted.

And then he made an offer, Lord—

An offer so attractive that I almost gave consent.

But it was all mixed up with sin and evil doing.

I didn't give in; I wanted to. I wavered, undecided,

I called Your name, and suddenly I had the strength to stand.

What happened, Lord?

PROMISE:

"There hath no temptation taken you but such as is common to man: but God is faithful, who will not suffer you to be tempted above that ye are able; but will with the temptation also make a way to escape, that ye may be able to bear it" I Cor. 10:13.

"The Lord knoweth how to deliver the godly out of temptations, and to reserve the unjust unto the day of judgment to be punished" II Peter 2:9.

"Resist the devil, and he will flee from you" James 4:7b.

6 ON BEING RESPONSIBLE

"Wherefore by their fruits ye shall know them" Matt. 7:20.

PRAYER:

Dear Lord, help me to accept responsibility.
I want to be the kind
   who does the job
   who runs the race
   who can be counted on.

You know the times that I've not carried through when others thought I would.

Why does my enthusiasm fade, and how can my promises so easily be forgotten?

I know it's wrong. I've sensed disgust and disappointment when I've let someone down.

How must I make You feel? You have counted on me, too.

Wake up my conscience, Lord, and help me be the one You can depend on.

PROMISE:

"Who then is the faithful, thoughtful and wise servant, whom his master has put in charge of his household, to give to the others the food and supplies at the proper time? Blessed . . . is that servant whom when his master comes he will find so doing" Matt. 24:45, 46, Amplified.

"Wherewithal shall a young man cleanse his way? by taking heed thereto according to thy word" Ps. 119:9.

"A faithful employee is as refreshing as a cool day in the hot summertime" Prov. 25:13, TLB.

7 COUNT TO TEN

"Anger resteth in the bosom of fools" Eccles. 7:9b.

PRAYER:

Dear Lord, my temper flared again. You see, I was irritated because I felt I was being wronged.

Quick as a flash I lost my sense of reason.

I said some hateful things, and I meant for them to hurt.

But I'm the one who's hurting now.

If only, Lord, I could recall each bitter word.

I'm ashamed that I lose control when I want so much to be like Christ.

I've said, "I'm sorry," but things are not the same. Relationships are strained and I am miserable.

Oh, God, forgive me. Help me control my temper.

PROMISE:

"Put off all these; anger, wrath, malice, blasphemy, filthy communication out of your mouth" Col. 3:8.

"Let every man be swift to hear, slow to speak, slow to wrath" James 1:19b.

"He that is slow to anger is better than the mighty; and he that ruleth his spirit than he that taketh a city" Prov. 16:32.

"Be ye angry, and sin not: let not the sun go down upon your wrath" Eph. 4:26.

8 ON BEING A COWARD

"Be not afraid, only believe" Mark 5:36b.

PRAYER:

Lord, I am such a coward!
If I had lived in Your day
   I would have run from the cross
   Hid from Your accusers
   Lied to the magistrates
I would have been just like Peter, denying . . .
But I live today, and it's the same old story
   I'm afraid to witness, even to my own family
   Or stand alone when friends ridicule
   Or when teachers question my beliefs
   I'm afraid to pray in public
   I hear Your name taken in vain and although I inwardly cringe, I remain passive.

Lord, please help.

PROMISE:

"Watch ye, stand fast in the faith, quit you like men, be strong" I Cor. 16:13.

"God hath not given us the spirit of fear; but of power, and of love, and of a sound mind. Be not thou therefore ashamed of the testimony of our Lord" II Tim. 1:7, 8a.

"Fear not them which kill the body, but are not able to kill the soul: but rather fear him which is able to destroy both soul and body in hell" Matt. 10:28.

9 NOBODY UNDERSTANDS ME

"Understanding is a wellspring of life unto him that hath it" Prov. 16:22a.

PRAYER:

Dear Lord, no one understands me.

There is not one person who cares enough to share my innermost thoughts.

Often I'm loneliest when surrounded by those I know the best.

I reach out, but no one reaches back.

No one cares about the real me.

I'm starved for understanding.

Do You know how I feel?

When You walked the earth and Your disciples failed to understand, was it like this?

When the rich young ruler turned away, did You feel sorrow, too?

And oh, the cross! The whole world turned its back on You!

Oh, Lord, I know You understand!

PROMISE:

"Him that cometh to me I will in no wise cast out" John 6:37b.

"As the Father hath loved me, so have I loved you: continue ye in my love" John 15:9.

"I am the bread of life: he that cometh to me shall never hunger; and he that believeth on me shall never thirst" John 6:35.

"Great is our Lord, and of great power: his understanding is infinite" Ps. 147:5.

10 THE GOSSIP ITCH

"Set a watch, O Lord, before my mouth; keep the door of my lips" Ps. 141:3.

PRAYER:

Oh, God, I really need You now
I know a secret bit of news
   It is not kind
   I *think* it's true
   I want to tell it so
I want my friend to gasp and say, "I thought so all the time. And did you know. . . ?"

How can I hold my tongue, dear Lord, today and every day?

PROMISE:

". . . Be thou an example of the believers, in word, in conversation. . ." I Tim. 4:12.

"If any man offend not in word, the same is a perfect man, and able also to bridle the whole body" James 3:2b.

"But I say unto you, that every idle word that men shall speak, they shall give account thereof in the day of judgment" Matt. 12:36.

"My prayer for you is that you will overflow more and more with love for others, and at the same time keep on growing in spiritual knowledge and insight" Phil. 1:9, TLB.

11 GOING THROUGH THE MOTIONS

"Then beware lest thou forget the Lord" Deut. 6:12a.

PRAYER:

I went to worship You, but Lord, I must confess that all I did was just go through the motions.

I stood to sing, but not one word had meaning. My voice did not ring out with joyful praise to You.

I bowed my head as if to pray, and then my mind went soaring off along some outdoor path.

We read Your Word; I closed my mind. My heart felt icy cold.

The preacher stood behind the sacred desk and spoke of Christ and His great love. And still it failed to reach me.

O Lord, is there an antidote for coldness?

PROMISE:

"If ye then be risen with Christ, seek those things which are above, where Christ sitteth on the right hand of God" Col. 3:1.

"Draw nigh to God, and he will draw nigh to you" James 4:8a.

"Love not the world, neither the things that are in the world. If any man love the world, the love of the Father is not in him" I John 2:15.

12 HEART HURT

"He healeth the broken in heart, and bindeth up their wounds" Ps. 147:3.

PRAYER:

Oh, Lord, I just met a new kind of hurt. Not a physical hurt, I could have taken that and now be healing. But it was a crushing blow and left a wound so big that I feel I will wear the scar forever.

My friend informed me that we're "through"; that from now on we'll go our separate ways. We've been inseparable for weeks. He said he'll date others and I am free to do the same. And then he said, "We'll still be friends."

Oh, Lord, my throat hurt so much I couldn't speak. My whole world crashed down around me. I thank You that I did not cry. But now, please speak some comfort to my heart. It's so hard to feel cast aside, that no one cares, and everyone at school and church is talking.

I need Your help today in a way that I have never needed it before. Please help me, Lord.

PROMISE:

"Cast thy burden upon the Lord, and he shall sustain thee" Ps. 55:22a.

"I will not leave you comfortless: I will come to you" John 14:18.

"Blessed be God, even the Father of our Lord Jesus Christ, the Father of mercies, and the God of all comfort; who comforteth us in all our tribulation" II Cor. 1:3, 4a.

13 FRUSTRATION

"I am thy servant; give me understanding, that I may know thy testimonies" Ps. 119:125.

PRAYER:

Dear Lord, there is so much frustration in my life.

My parents say that I'm too young for this, too old for that.

Someone tells me, "You wouldn't understand!"

I don't know how to act in many situations. Often I'm embarrassed.

I speak with certainty about a question in debate and later find that I was wrong. And then I feel so agonizingly foolish.

Is this a part of growing up? Lord, please help me overcome these feelings of frustration.

PROMISE:

"Don't let anyone think little of you because you are young. Be their ideal; let them follow the way you teach and live; be a pattern for them in your love, your faith, and your clean thoughts" I Tim. 4:12, TLB.

"Be strong and of a good courage; be not afraid, neither be thou dismayed: for the Lord thy God is with thee whithersoever thou goest" Josh. 1:9.

"Remember now thy Creator in the days of thy youth" Eccles. 12:1a.

14 PEER PRESSURE

"My son, if sinners entice thee, consent thou not" Prov. 1:10.

PRAYER:

Dear Lord, there is so much social drinking among my friends.

And even younger kids are getting involved.

"Just one little drink," they insist, and then argue in its favor.

At every party at my school there is someone with a bottle.

But Lord, I've driven by skid row and I've seen what drinking can lead to.

Please, God, give me an answer for this growing problem.

PROMISE:

"Whose heart is filled with anguish and sorrow? Who is always fighting and quarreling? Who is the man with bloodshot eyes and many wounds? It is the one who spends long hours in the taverns, trying out new mixtures. Don't let the sparkle and the smooth taste of strong wine deceive you. For in the end it bites like a poisonous serpent; it stings like an adder" Prov. 23:29-32, TLB.

"And be not conformed to this world: but be ye transformed by the renewing of your mind, that ye may prove what is that good, and acceptable, and perfect, will of God" Rom. 12:2.

"Be not deceived; God is not mocked: for whatsoever a man soweth, that shall he also reap" Gal. 6:7.

15 A SERMON WITHOUT WORDS

"Let your light so shine before men, that they may see your good works, and glorify your Father which is in heaven" Matt. 5:16.

PRAYER:

Lord, I keep forgetting that Christians are often sermons without words.

I find it hard to remember that some of my non-believing friends may judge all Christians by me.

Or that those who never open Your Word expect me to be a walking Bible because I've identified myself with You.

I've heard how the "hypocrites in the church" keep so many people from coming.

Oh, Lord, it's too much for me alone. I can only help if I live my life through You.

PROMISE:

"Brethren, be followers together of me, and mark them which walk so as ye have us for an ensample" Phil. 3:17.

"I am crucified with Christ: nevertheless I live; yet not I, but Christ liveth in me: and the life which I now live in the flesh I live by the faith of the Son of God, who loved me, and gave himself for me" Gal. 2:20.

"Be ye stedfast, unmoveable, always abounding in the work of the Lord, forasmuch as ye know that your labour is not in vain in the Lord" I Cor. 15:58.

16 LEFT OUT

"The eyes of the Lord are upon the righteous, and his ears are open unto their cry" Ps. 34:15.

PRAYER:

Dear Lord, I've been left out. You see, there was a party and I was not invited. My friends were there, but no one included me.

I've searched my heart to find out why, for there must be a reason—
- have I not turned my other cheek
- or gone a second mile
- or ever looked for good in those with whom I disagree?
- have I not loved enough, my Lord, when others were in pain?
- have I thought too much of "me" and sought to have my way?

Lord, I know You were left out, too, when You walked earth's dusty trails, but not for these reasons. But didn't it hurt, as it hurts me?

PROMISE:

"We can rejoice, too, when we run into problems and trials for we know that they are good for us—they help us learn to be patient. And patience develops strength of character in us and helps us trust God more each time we use it until finally our hope and faith are strong and steady. Then, when that happens, we are able to hold our heads high no matter what happens and know that all is well, for we know how dearly God loves us" Rom. 5:3-5a, TLB.

17 A THOUSAND FEARS

"Trust ye in the Lord for ever: for in the Lord Jehovah is everlasting strength" Isa. 26:4.

PRAYER:

Dear Lord, I am afraid. So many frightening things unsettle me—

> the noises in the night, strange and alarming
> the storms, when winds blow strong and destruction seems imminent
> crime, that reaches into our peaceful neighborhood
> disturbances in my school and on the college campus
> the constant threat of war (will I be involved?)
> the economic situation, and what it will do to my future

Dear Lord, is it possible for me to overcome my fears?

PROMISE:

"Commit thy way unto the Lord; trust also in him; and he shall bring it to pass" Ps. 37:5.

"We are pressed on every side by troubles, but not crushed and broken. We are perplexed because we don't know why things happen as they do, but we don't give up and quit. We are hunted down, but God never abandons us. We get knocked down, but we get up again and keep going. These bodies of ours are constantly facing death just as Jesus did; so it is clear to all that it is only the living Christ within [who keeps us safe]" II Cor. 4:8-10, TLB.

"The Lord is good, a strong hold in the day of trouble; and he knoweth them that trust in him" Nah. 1:7.

18 SOMEONE'S CRYING, LORD

"Whatsoever ye shall ask in my name, that will I do, that the Father may be glorified in the Son" John 14:13.

PRAYER:

Dear Lord, there are so many who are hurting, and I feel so helpless.

I know a girl who is pregnant; her boy friend ran away.

There's a boy in my school who is already on drugs, and he's younger than I am.

An elderly lady lives near me, alone, and her monthly income won't meet all of her needs.

I know a beautiful child with golden hair—and blind eyes.

There are so many crying, Lord, and I cry with them.

Please extend Your hand of comfort.

PROMISE:

"My grace is sufficient for thee: for my strength is made perfect in weakness" II Cor. 12:9a.

"Call unto me, and I will answer thee, and shew thee great and mighty things, which thou knowest not" Jer. 33:3.

"Be of good courage, and he shall strengthen your heart, all ye that hope in the Lord" Ps. 31:24.

"Surely he hath borne our griefs, and carried our sorrows" Isa. 53:4a.

19 PRIDE

"Pride goeth before destruction, and an haughty spirit before a fall" Prov. 16:18.

PRAYER:

Oh, Lord, You know how I love to be seen in all of the right places. And how I let everyone know all of my accomplishments. And how I mention names and places to impress my friends.

My life is a mirror which reflects my prideful inner self.

Tonight I've turned Your searchlight on myself. I admit I don't like what I see.

If I don't like what I see in myself, how can others like me?

And Lord, how do I look to You?

How can I keep myself from pride and all of its added problems?

PROMISE:

"Quit acting so proud and arrogant! The Lord knows what you have done, and he will judge your deeds" I Sam. 2:3, TLB.

"If we confess our sins, he is faithful and just to forgive us our sins, and to cleanse us from all unrighteousness" I John 1:9.

"Praise the Lord; for the Lord is good: sing praises unto his name; for it is pleasant" Ps. 135:3.

20 BROKEN PROMISES

"Create in me a clean heart, O God; and renew a right spirit within me" Ps. 51:10.

PRAYER:

I have broken a promise, Lord. I am ashamed and sorry.

I always thought my word was good, that I could be depended on.

I can't explain it, really.

I slipped—and fell—now I'm contrite

I'm afraid my friends won't ever trust me again.

What can I do to restore their faith in me?

PROMISE:

"Anyone willing to be corrected is on the pathway to life. Anyone refusing has lost his chance" Prov. 10:17, TLB.

"In all things shewing thyself a pattern of good works: in doctrine shewing uncorruptness, gravity, sincerity, sound speech, that cannot be condemned; that he that is of the contrary part may be ashamed, having no evil thing to say of you" Titus 2:7, 8.

"Be not a witness against thy neighbour without cause; and deceive not with thy lips" Prov. 24:28.

21 JOY BEHIND THE WHEEL

"The Lord is my strength and my shield" Ps. 28:7a.

PRAYER:

Dear Lord, at last the time has come when I can drive the car alone.

I thank You that I passed the tests and now I'm on my own.

I feel so independent; I've wanted this for months,

But deep inside I'm frightened, too.

I'm not as confident as I appear—

Although I show off now and then—

Please ride with me behind the wheel, and give me driving sense

(I'm quick to panic, Lord)

And Father, never, never, let me be involved in any tragedy.

PROMISE:

"The Lord is their strength, and he is the saving strength of his anointed" Ps. 28:8.

"The good man does not escape all troubles—he has them too. But the Lord helps him in each and every one. God even protects him from accidents" Ps. 34:19, 20, TLB.

"For he shall give his angels charge over thee, to keep thee in all thy ways" Ps. 91:11.

22 ON BEING A FRIEND

"A friend loveth at all times" Prov. 17:17a.

PRAYER:

Dear Lord, I'm afraid I just lost a friend, one that I really love.

I gave her some honest criticism (she asked me what I thought).

My judgment must have sounded harsh, for she became furious.

Why didn't I speak more kindly?

The issue was only a minor one, merely a matter of taste.

Why didn't I use more tact?

Again I cry for help, Lord. Sometimes I hate myself.

PROMISE:

"Dear brothers, don't be too eager to tell others their faults, for we all make many mistakes" James 3:1, TLB.

"Steer clear of foolish discussions which lead people into the sin of anger with each other" II Tim. 2:16, TLB.

"A man that hath friends must shew himself friendly: and there is a friend that sticketh closer than a brother" Prov. 18:24.

"Ye are my friends, if ye do whatsoever I command you" John 15:14.

23 DISAPPOINTMENT DILEMMA

"In the day when I cried thou answeredst me, and strengthenedst me with strength in my soul" Ps. 138:3.

PRAYER:

Oh, Lord, I'm deeply disappointed; my best friend has won the award I hoped to win.

I worked so hard to have it for my own. I prayed; I hoped, but all for nothing.

Now it is hers.

How can I say, "I'm glad for you?" when I really feel like crying? How can I hide the bitter disappointment that crushes me inside?

Oh, my Father, help me to swallow tears and hurt and grow a little taller.

I beg You, Lord, to help.

PROMISE:

"Don't just pretend that you love others: really love them. Hate what is wrong. Stand on the side of the good. Love each other with brotherly affection and take delight in honoring each other" Rom. 12:9, 10, TLB.

"When others are happy, be happy with them. If they are sad, share their sorrow" Rom. 12:15, TLB.

"In response to all he has done for us, let us outdo each other in being helpful and kind to each other and in doing good" Heb. 10:24, TLB.

24 PROCRASTINATION

"I must work the works of him that sent me, while it is day: the night cometh, when no man can work" John 9:4.

PRAYER:

Dear Lord, I put things off.

I have such good intentions; I have some big ideas, and I even have a list of things to do.

But I lack the drive—the discipline—the will-power—the time.

Help me to overcome my weakness, Lord.

I start so many things and they stare back at me, unfinished.

How can I conquer this fault?

PROMISE:

"Be diligent that ye may be found of him in peace, without spot, and blameless" II Peter 3:14b.

"Whatsoever thy hand findeth to do, do it with thy might" Eccles. 9:10a.

"For God shall bring every work into judgment, with every secret thing, whether it be good, or whether it be evil" Eccles. 12:14.

"Commit thy works unto the Lord, and thy thoughts shall be established" Prov. 16:3.

25 PRONE

"For the good that I would I do not: but the evil which I would not, that I do" Rom. 7:19.

PRAYER:

Oh, Lord, why am I so prone—
- to criticize when I don't know all of the facts
- to feel smug when I'm not guilty of someone else's sin
- to look down in fear when I should look up in faith
- to speak my piece when silence would indeed be golden?

Why do I do these things when I honestly know better and long to be more like Christ?

PROMISE:

"Those who let themselves be controlled by their lower natures live only to please themselves, but those who follow after the Holy Spirit find themselves doing those things that please God" Rom. 8:5, TLB.

"There is therefore now no condemnation to them which are in Christ Jesus, who walk not after the flesh, but after the Spirit" Rom. 8:1.

"Keep thy heart with all diligence; for out of it are the issues of life" Prov. 4:23.

26 SPANKING FROM HEAVEN

"Wash me throughly from mine iniquity, and cleanse me from my sin" Ps. 51:2.

PRAYER:

Dear Father, I feel Your chastening hand today, and I know why.

I sinned and I deserve it.

Forgive me. I knew my action was wrong, and now I feel the sting of guilt. My head bows with shame.

I know that You are trying to shape and mold me to be like Christ. And I'm so stubborn.

Correction isn't pleasant, but I know I need it, Lord.

Even as I suffer, I'm glad You really care.

PROMISE:

"Let God train you, for he is doing what any loving father does for his children. Whoever heard of a son who was never corrected? If God doesn't punish you when you need it, as other fathers punish their sons, then it means that you aren't really God's son at all—that you don't really belong in his family" Heb. 12:7, 8, TLB.

"For whom the Lord loveth, he chasteneth" Heb. 12:6a.

"Your iniquities have separated between you and your God, and your sins have hid his face from you, that he will not hear" Isa. 59:2.

27 BROKEN-HEARTED

"In my distress I cried unto the Lord, and he heard me" Ps. 120:1.

PRAYER:

Oh, my Father, I love him, but he doesn't love You. It hurts me to think it—he doesn't love You!
> Your Son is a stranger to him
> the cross, he sees as a worthless sacrifice
> there is no hope of Heaven in his heart,
> no comfort in the night,
> no strength for things to come,

I plead with him; I pray. My tears do no good.
He only laughs at me.

It seems I cannot give him up, and yet, deep in my heart I know that we must part.

O God! I love him, but I love You more!

PROMISE:

"Be ye not unequally yoked together with unbelievers" II Cor. 6:14a.

"If a man love me, he will keep my words: and my Father will love him, and we will come unto him, and make our abode with him" John 14:23.

"Thou wilt keep him in perfect peace, whose mind is stayed on thee: because he trusteth in thee" Isa. 26:3.

28 ACCORDING TO YOUR PLAN

"This one thing I do, forgetting those things which are behind, and reaching forth unto those things which are before" Phil. 3:13b.

PRAYER:

How can I know the right road you've planned for me, Lord? All paths seem to lie straight ahead.

Yet one must be Your perfect will for me.

I want the very center of Your plan for all my life. I do not care where it leads as long as You are there.

There are so many roads, I can't be sure which one You mean for me to take.

Please show me, Lord, for Jesus' sake.

PROMISE:

"I beseech you therefore, brethren, by the mercies of God, that ye present your bodies a living sacrifice, holy, acceptable unto God, which is your reasonable service" Rom. 12:1.

"Blessed is the man that walketh not in the counsel of the ungodly, nor standeth in the way of sinners, nor sitteth in the seat of the scornful" Ps. 1:1.

"Set your affection on things above, not on things on the earth" Col. 3:2.

29 ON DILIGENCE

"Seest thou a man diligent in his business? he shall stand before kings" Prov. 22:29a.

PRAYER:

Dear Lord, these are days when nothing happens. My life drifts idly by.

Everywhere I go things are the same; there's nothing exciting for me to do.

My friends feel it, too, and so we do "nothing" together.

My parents lecture. I hear them say—we're "lazy," and "aimless," we have "too much leisure;" we'll "get into trouble" and "amount to nothing."

But truthfully, I'm bored. How can I overcome this state of lethargy?

I ask in Jesus' name.

PROMISE:

"He that gathereth in summer is a wise son: but he that sleepeth in harvest is a son that causeth shame" Prov. 10:5.

"Study to be quiet, and to do your own business, and to work with your own hands, as we commanded you" I Thess. 4:11.

"So be careful how you act; these are difficult days. Don't be fools; be wise: make the most of every opportunity you have for doing good" Eph. 5:15, 16, TLB.

"Yet we hear that some of you are living in laziness, refusing to work, and wasting your time in gossiping. In the name of the Lord Jesus Christ we appeal to such people—we command them—to quiet down, get to work, and earn their own living" II Thess. 3:11, 12, TLB.

30 ONE TALENT MAN

"Unto one he gave five talents, to another two, and to another one" Matt. 25:15a.

PRAYER:

Dear Lord, You have given me a talent—
   a precious thing to use for You
   a generous gift, my Master
   one that You want me to take and use to show Your love.

I know I must work to develop it, but I am lazy and afraid.

I tried to bury it in the ground, just like the unfaithful servant in the parable. But now I come to You, ashamed.

When I have taken my talent from its secret place and shown it to the world, I have received encouragement and praise.

That has been sweet to my ego, and made me want to develop my talent further. But I am lazy, Lord.

Today at last I have decided I want to make this gift into one I can use for Your glory.

Am I too late?

Please keep today's enthusiasm burning in my heart.

PROMISE:

"Every branch in me that beareth not fruit he taketh away: and every branch that beareth fruit, he purgeth it, that it may bring forth more fruit" John 15:2.

"The man who uses well what he is given shall be given more, and he shall have abundance" Matt. 25:29a, TLB.

31 SILENCE FROM HEAVEN

"Why art thou cast down, O my soul?" Ps. 43:5a.

PRAYER:

Lord, You keep saying, "No" and I don't understand why.

The things I want would not be hard for You to give—

>You own the cattle on a thousand hills
>You have the power to still the storm
>You are able to heal the sick

Why can't I have what I want, Lord?
Is it not best for me to have those things?
Don't they fit into Your plan for my life?
Do You have something better for me, Lord?

Oh, give me the patience to wait and see.

PROMISE:

"Ye ask, and receive not, because ye ask amiss, that ye may consume it upon your lusts" James 4:3.

"Now we know that God heareth not sinners: but if any man be a worshipper of God, and doeth his will, him he heareth" John 9:31.

"The Spirit also helpeth our infirmities: for we know not what we should pray for as we ought: but the Spirit itself maketh intercession for us with groanings which cannot be uttered" Rom. 8:26.

32 WHICH WAY, LORD?

"Order my steps in thy word: and let not any iniquity have dominion over me" Ps. 119:133.

PRAYER:

Dear Lord, my heart is in a turmoil. I feel delighted, but at the same time I'm half-afraid.

I've been offered a job. It sounds so exciting, but it will make a big change in my life.

Even though I see all the opportunity it would bring, I want to make sure I accept the offer only if it is Your will.

If this job would lessen our closeness; if it would lead me away from You or bring disgrace to Your name in any way, please close the door. (I cannot see the future, but it is known to You.)

For now, unless You intervene, I'll move ahead. It comforts me to know that You care enough to close and open doors and guide me in the choices I must make.

Lord, if You do say "No" help me to accept your answer with maturity.

PROMISE:

"If thy presence go not with me, carry us not up hence" Exod. 33:15.

"The eyes of the Lord are over the righteous, and his ears are open unto their prayers" I Peter 3:12a.

"Wherefore be ye not unwise, but understanding what the will of the Lord is" Eph. 5:17.

33 SOMETHING FOR YOU

"Unless the Lord had been my help, my soul had almost dwelt in silence" Ps. 94:17.

PRAYER:

Dear Lord, I have nothing to bring to You—
- no bird-like song in my throat to inspire a listening crowd,
- no nimble fingers on the flute to soothe those full of worries and tensions,

and when I stand to speak, I tremble, Lord.
I do not have an artist's touch, nor an author's way with words,
I try to witness but my tongue is tied.
Yet deep inside, I long to have a gift that I can bring.

What is there, Lord, that I can do for You?

PROMISE:

"On the good ground are they, which in an honest and good heart, having heard the word, keep it, and bring forth fruit with patience" Luke 8:15.

"Give unto the Lord the glory due unto his name: bring an offering, and come before him: worship the Lord in the beauty of holiness" I Chron. 16:29.

"You younger men, follow the leadership of those who are older. And all of you serve each other with humble spirits, for God gives special blessings to those who are humble, but sets himself against those who are proud" I Peter 5:5, TLB.

34 SUCCESS STORY

"For even the Son of man came not to be ministered unto, but to minister, and to give his life a ransom for many" Mark 10:45.

PRAYER:

Dear Lord, You have invited us to come boldly before Your throne.

Today I come to ask You for guidance for my future.

Adults wish me success in life, but Lord, I want to know what *You* consider to be true success.

I know that some men—lots of them, I think—measure it by wealth, fame or political glory.

I don't want to live my life for these things and find in the end that I've missed Your blessing.

Please make it plain to me before I set the wrong goals.

What is a successful life?

PROMISE:

"But he that is greatest among you shall be your servant. And whosoever shall exalt himself shall be abased; and he that shall humble himself shall be exalted" Matt. 23:11, 12.

"For whosoever will save his life shall lose it; but whosoever shall lose his life for my sake and the gospel's, the same shall save it. For what shall it profit a man, if he shall gain the whole world, and lose his own soul?" Mark 8:35, 36.

"Some rich people are poor, and some poor people have great wealth!" Prov. 13:7, TLB.

35 AN ARGUMENT

"Let brotherly love continue" Heb. 13:1.

PRAYER:

I've tried for weeks to reach my friend for You.

But, Lord, I was a shameful witness.

I don't know how it happened, but we got into an argument about the virgin birth. I wanted so to win!

I spoke with great authority (because I know I'm right)—

I can't understand why I could not convince my friend, since this is such an important truth.

Help me to share Your Word as You would want me to.

PROMISE:

"If I speak with the tongues of men and of angels, but have not love, I am become sounding brass, or a clanging cymbal" I Cor. 13:1, ASV.

"Love as brethren, be pitiful, be courteous" I Peter 3:8b.

"And this commandment have we from him, That he who loveth God love his brother also" I John 4:21.

"A soft answer turneth away wrath: but grievous words stir up anger" Prov. 15:1.

36 THE HONOR SYSTEM

"In the way of righteousness is life" Prov. 12:28a.

PRAYER:

Dear Lord, I'm so concerned about the cheating in my school.

Even a lot of "good kids" are involved.

Some teachers put us on our "honor" but it's nothing but a farce.

Copies of exams are passed around; it's so hard not to look at them.

We need high grades for
> scholarships,
>> parents' approval
>>> status with our friends, and
>>>> special privileges.

What advantage is there in trying to be honest?

Show me again how wrong cheating is, Lord, so I, too, won't fall into this trap.

PROMISE:

"The Lord hates cheating and delights in honesty" Prov. 11:1, TLB.

"Winking at sin leads to sorrow; bold reproof leads to peace" Prov. 10:10, TLB.

"Who may stand before the Lord? Only those with pure hands and hearts, who do not practice dishonesty and lying" Ps. 24:3b, 4, TLB.

37 ON GIVING

"For the love of money is the root of all evil" I Tim. 6:10a.

PRAYER:

Dear Lord, thank You for helping me find a job.

And thank You for letting me have my own money.

Please help me to have good judgment in using it—I find it so easy to overspend!

And, oh, I know a part of it belongs to You.

Forgive me for wanting—sometimes—to keep Your part for myself.

Help me remember the widow and her two mites.

Help me remember how You give and give and give!

Lord, give me a generous heart.

PROMISE:

"God loveth a cheerful giver" II Cor. 9:7b.

"It is more blessed to give than to receive" Acts 20:35b.

"On every Lord's Day each of you should put aside something from what you have earned during the week, and use it for this offering. The amount depends on how much the Lord has helped you earn" I Cor. 16:2a, TLB.

"Bring ye all the tithes into the storehouse, that there may be meat in mine house, and prove me now herewith, saith the Lord of hosts, if I will not open you the windows of heaven, and pour you out a blessing, that there shall not be room enough to receive it" Mal. 3:10.

38 ME? AN EXAMPLE?

"But God had mercy on me so that Christ Jesus could use me as an example to show everyone how patient he is with even the worst sinners, so that others will realize that they, too, can have everlasting life" I Tim. 1:16, TLB.

PRAYER:

Dear Lord, help me to be a good example.

I want to show that Jesus has made a big change in my life.

I've tried to tell my friends what He has done for me, but some of them look at me with raised eyebrows, as if to say, "We'll wait and see."

I'm trying, Lord. I've had to bite my tongue at times to stop a sharp reply.

And once I caught myself before I stretched the truth.

I criticize so easily, and my temper is short.

But You've promised to help me overcome these things.

Oh, help me, Lord!

PROMISE:

"For I have given you an example, that ye should do as I have done to you" John 13:15.

"Try to stay out of all quarrels and seek to live a clean and holy life, for one who is not holy will not see the Lord" Heb. 12:14, TLB.

"Abstain from all appearance of evil" I Thess. 5:22.

"Wherefore, if meat make my brother to offend, I will eat no flesh while the world standeth, lest I make my brother to offend" I Cor. 8:13.

39 PLAYING HOOKY

"Not forsaking the assembling of ourselves together, as the manner of some is" Heb. 10:25a.

PRAYER:

Yesterday was Sunday, Lord, and I stayed home.
I did not go to Your sacred house to worship You.
After all, I almost had a headache and my eyes were tired. I really needed sleep, Lord—I know You understand.
Besides, I'm tired of all the hypocrites at church.
I told my parents I would worship alone at home.
The week is wearing on, and now I find some things I hadn't anticipated.

> I've eaten, but I'm hungry, Lord, deep down inside;
> No joyful songs fill my heart;
> I've read Your word, but I couldn't understand it.
> My body has rested, but my spirit is still restless.

What is so special about going to church?

PROMISE:

"... Christ also loved the church, and gave himself for it" Eph. 5:25b.

"And hath put all things under his feet, and gave him to be the head over all things to the church, which is his body" Eph. 1:22, 23a.

"A single day spent in your Temple is better than a thousand anywhere else!" Ps. 84:10a, TLB.

"And he came to Nazareth, where he had been brought up: and, as his custom was, he went into the synagogue on the sabbath day" Luke 4:16.

40 "I'LL BE A WITNESS..."

"And they that be wise shall shine as the brightness of the firmament; and they that turn many to righteousness as the stars for ever and ever" Dan. 12:3.

PRAYER:

I love You, Lord, with my whole heart.
I love You because of what You have done for me.
> You made a way for me to escape the punishment I deserve for my sin.
> You brought me to the foot of the cross and opened my eyes to the sacrifice Jesus made there.
> You cleansed my heart.
> You made a new person out of me.

I want to share my experience, but fear holds me back.
> I try to speak, but words won't come.
> My mouth gets dry.
> My tongue insists on getting twisted.

How can I be a witness for You, Lord?

PROMISE:

"Praise the Lord, call upon his name, declare his doings among the people, make mention that his name is exalted" Isa. 12:4b.

"Whosoever heareth these sayings of mine, and doeth them, I will liken him unto a wise man, which built his house upon a rock" Matt. 7:24.

"Finally, my brethren, be strong in the Lord, and in the power of his might. Put on the whole armour of God, that ye may be able to stand against the wiles of the devil" Eph. 6:10, 11.

41 ABOUT COVETING

"Let your conversation be without covetousness; and be content with such things as ye have" Heb. 13:5a.

PRAYER:

Oh, Lord, the word "covet" scares me.
It speaks of selfishness and greed,
    priorities out of focus,
        desires out of control.
And smugly, I thought I was exempt from those faults—until yesterday.
Yesterday I had a strong desire to own something my friend owns.
Not a gentle, soft wanting, but a fierce craving.
I am not tempted, Lord, to steal (I'm not a thief) but what I desire costs more money than I have.
My mind has done some quiet scheming—
    can I borrow from a friend?
    or secretly use my mother's credit card?
    or ask for an advance on my allowance?
    or skip my church gift for a while?

Please, God, straighten me out before I get into water so deep that I will never make it to the shore.

PROMISE:

"Beware! Don't always be wishing for what you don't have. For real life and real living are not related to how rich we are" Luke 12:15, TLB.

"Thou shalt not covet" Exod. 20:17a.

"Some men enjoy cheating, but the cake they buy with such ill-gotten gain will turn to gravel in their mouths" Prov. 20:17, TLB.

42 DOES ANYTHING GO?

"For the ways of man are before the eyes of the Lord, and he pondereth all his goings" Prov. 5:21.

PRAYER:

Dear Lord, there is so much promiscuousness among my friends—easy sex, self-gratification, pleasure for pleasure's sake.

I've been laughed at because my moral code says sex is sacred.

Some friends say that I am missing what life is all about, that I'm old-fashioned and quixotic in my thinking.

My heart tells me to wait. I want to enter marriage pure and undefiled.

But my friends try to cloud the issue; they are persuasive.

Oh, Lord, help me to know that I am thinking straight.

PROMISE:

"For from the heart come evil thoughts, murder, adultery, fornication, theft, lying and slander. These are what defile" Matt. 15:19, 20a, TLB.

"But clothe yourself with the Lord Jesus Christ, the Messiah, and make no provision for (indulging) the flesh—put a stop to thinking about the evil cravings of your physical nature—to (gratify its) desires (lusts)" Rom. 13:14, Amplified.

"My son, attend unto my wisdom, and bow thine ear to my understanding: that thou mayest regard discretion, and that thy lips may keep knowledge" Prov. 5:1, 2.

43 OVERCOMING WORRY

"The just shall live by his faith" Hab. 2:4b.

PRAYER:

Dear Father, I thank You for offering to all of Your children a *life of faith*.

I know if I exercise this gift I will have freedom from one of my big problems—*worry!*

Why do I act as if You don't exist, the way atheists do?

And why do I torture myself with doubts, when faith would cover a multitude of problems?

And often, Lord, the things that I worry about most never happen.

Help me to overcome my anxiety.

PROMISE:

"So don't be anxious about tomorrow. God will take care of your tomorrow too. Live one day at a time" Matt. 6:34, TLB.

"But Jesus turned him about, and when he saw her, he said, Daughter, be of good comfort; thy faith hath made thee whole" Matt. 9:22a.

"The Lord says: Cursed is the man who puts his trust in mortal man and turns his heart away from God. He is like a stunted shrub in the desert, with no hope for the future; he lives on the salt-encrusted plains in the barren wilderness; good times pass him by forever" Jer. 17:5, 6 TLB.

44 NO SKEPTIC HERE

"For the preaching of the cross is to them that perish foolishness" I Cor 1:18a.

PRAYER:

Lord, many people don't believe in You at my school, and this disturbs me.

Some students, and even some teachers, seem confused and skeptical.

Some claim that You do not exist.

They doubt creation's lovely dawn.

They explain away the miracles.

They don't believe in Christ's atoning death or in His sure return.

I do not doubt You, Lord. What can I do to help?

PROMISE:

"Have faith in God" Mark 11:22b.

"And be ready always to give an answer to every man that asketh you a reason of the hope that is in you with meekness and fear" I Peter 3:15b.

"Let us hold fast the profession of our faith without wavering; (for he is faithful that promised)" Heb. 10:23.

"Ye therefore, beloved, seeing ye know these things before, beware lest ye also, being led away with the error of the wicked, fall from your own stedfastness" II Peter 3:17.

45 HOW DID IT ALL BEGIN?

"In the beginning God created the heaven and the earth" Gen. 1:1.

PRAYER:

Dear God, I look around and I am held in awe.

I see You in the mountains, so majestic from the plain,

Your hand has touched the waters and made them sparkling blue,

You paint a glorious picture in each sunset's brilliant hue,

The flowers, the trees, the restful green of grass and shrubbery, too,

And then the sky, a constant, changing panoramic view.

Tell me again how it all came to be.

PROMISE:

"Through faith we understand that the worlds were framed by the word of God, so that things which are seen were not made of things which do appear" Heb. 11:3.

"But we know that there is only one God, the Father, who created all things and made us to be his own; and one Lord Jesus Christ, who made everything and gives us life" I Cor. 8:6, TLB.

"Let everyone in all the world—men, women and children—fear the Lord and stand in awe of him. For when he but spoke, the world began! It appeared at his command!" Ps. 33:8, 9, TLB.

"Now in these days he has spoken to us through his Son to whom he has given everything, and through whom he made the world and everything there is" Heb. 1:2, TLB.

46 THE HOLY SPIRIT

"Not by might, nor by power, but by my spirit, saith the Lord of hosts" Zech. 4:6b.

PRAYER:

Heavenly Father, thank You for Your gift of the Holy Spirit. He does so much for me.

He pricks my conscience and makes me hurt inside when I've done wrong.

He opens up Your Word until the truths hit me between the eyes.

He helps me speak Your Word to others.

He fills my heart—a full cup of love.

He takes my faltering prayers before Your throne.

He makes my life amount to something.

Father, help me never, never to quench Your Holy Spirit.

PROMISE:

"Jesus answered, Verily, verily, I say unto thee, Except a man be born of water and of the Spirit, he cannot enter into the kingdom of God" John 3:5.

"Howbeit when he, the Spirit of truth, is come, he will guide you into all truth: for he shall not speak of himself; but whatsoever he shall hear, that shall he speak: and he will shew you things to come" John 16:13.

"Ye shall receive power, after that the Holy Ghost is come upon you" Acts 1:8a.

"But the fruit of the Spirit is love, joy, peace, longsuffering, gentleness, goodness, faith, meekness, temperance: against such there is no law" Gal. 5:22, 23.

47 AN AWFUL THOUGHT

"The way of life is above to the wise, that he may depart from hell beneath" Prov. 15:24.

PRAYER:

O God, the thought of never reaching Heaven just gripped me and I became paralyzed, immobile. The idea chilled me deep inside.

> Never to look at Your face?
> Never to fall at Your feet with my own personal adoration?
> Never to see my loved ones again?

I feel that death is but a door of darkness through which we all must pass, but only for a moment until all will be light.

Darkness forever? I cannot comprehend the awful meaning.

But even as I contemplate this horror, You give me peace again. And oh, I thank you, Lord, for this.

I know whom I have believed; but what of those who don't? My friends? Those close to me?

Oh, Father, what shall I tell them?

PROMISE:

"He that believeth on the Son hath everlasting life" John 3:36a.

"He that believeth on him is not condemned: but he that believeth not is condemned already, because he hath not believed in the name of the only begotten Son of God" John 3:18.

48 ALL POWERFUL

"What is man, that thou art mindful of him?" Ps. 8:4a.

PRAYER:

O God, I marvel at Your power! All power is Yours!
With a word You can still the storm
Or hush a baby's cry.
You spoke and the worlds were formed!
And man is Your creation.
You put the song in the throat of the bird,
You clothed the lilies of the field,
And oh, You made a plan to save my soul!

Dear God, I kneel in awe and wonder!

PROMISE:

"Thou, even thou, art Lord alone; thou hast made heaven, the heaven of heavens, with all their host, the earth, and all things that are therein, the seas, and all that is therein, and thou preservest them all; and the host of heaven worshippeth thee" Neh. 9:6.

"And one cried unto another, and said, Holy, holy, holy, is the Lord of hosts: the whole earth is full of his glory" Isa. 6:3.

"But the Lord is the true God, he is the living God, and an everlasting king" Jer. 10:10a.

"Heaven is my throne, and earth is my footstool" Acts 7:49a.

"Jesus ... said unto them, With men this is impossible; but with God all things are possible" Matt. 19:26.

49 PRESENT EVERYWHERE

"If I take the wings of the morning, and dwell in the uttermost parts of the sea; even there shall thy hand lead me, and thy right hand shall hold me" Ps. 139:9, 10.

PRAYER:

Thank You for Your omnipresence, Lord—
> You are always near when I call,
> there is never a "Closed" sign in the window,
> no one ever tells me You are "too busy" or "in conference."
> Your arm is extended in welcome,
> Your ear is willing to listen,
> Your love fills my soul.

I just wanted to tell You again, Lord, that You mean so much to me.

PROMISE:

"The eyes of the Lord run to and fro throughout the whole earth, to shew himself strong in the behalf of them whose heart is perfect toward him" II Chron. 16:9a.

"The eternal God is thy refuge, and underneath are the everlasting arms" Deut. 33:27a.

"The Lord is nigh unto all them that call upon him, to all that call upon him in truth" Ps. 145:18.

"The eyes of the Lord are in every place, beholding the evil and the good" Prov. 15:3.

50 ALL KNOWING

"For if our heart condemn us, God is greater than our heart, and knoweth all things" I John 3:20.

PRAYER:

O God, I cannot comprehend that *everything* is known to You—
> You know how many hairs are on each head,
> You even know when a sparrow falls,
> You are aware of every good, every evil, each tiny thing in Your creation.
> You know man's thoughts, before he thinks them,
> You see each heart, and its response to You,
> and You know all about me, personally.

Is it really true? Must I be afraid?

PROMISE:

"O the depth of the riches both of the wisdom and knowledge of God! how unsearchable are his judgments, and his ways past finding out!" Rom. 11:33.

"But the wisdom that is from above is first pure, then peaceable, gentle, and easy to be intreated, full of mercy and good fruits, without partiality, and without hypocrisy" James 3:17.

"Shall not God search this out? for he knoweth the secrets of the heart" Ps. 44:21.

"Don't you yet understand? Don't you know by now that the everlasting God, the Creator of the farthest parts of the earth, never grows faint or weary? No one can fathom the depths of his understanding" Isa. 40:28, TLB.

51 HE WILL COME AGAIN

". . . ye shall see the Son of man sitting on the right hand of power, and coming in the clouds of heaven" Mark 14:62.

PRAYER:

Dear Lord, I hear so much about Your return.
Sometimes I am afraid. And I have questions, too.
> Are You coming soon? Some people say You are.
> What are the signs that I should watch for?
> Will I know You when You come?
> How will it all take place?

Oh, Lord, how can I know that I'll be ready?

PROMISE:

"And there shall be signs in the sun, and in the moon, and in the stars; and upon the earth distress of nations, with perplexity; the sea and the waves roaring; Men's hearts failing them for fear, and for looking after those things which are coming on the earth: for the powers of heaven shall be shaken. And then shall they see the Son of man coming in a cloud with power and great glory" Luke 21:25-27.

"For the Lord himself shall descend from heaven with a shout, with the voice of the archangel, and with the trump of God: and the dead in Christ shall rise first: Then we which are alive and remain shall be caught up together with them in the clouds to meet the Lord in the air: and so shall we ever be with the Lord" I Thess. 4:16, 17.

"And they said, Believe on the Lord Jesus Christ, and thou shalt be saved, and thy house" Acts 16:31.

52 SATISFIED

"For whosoever shall call upon the name of the Lord shall be saved" Rom. 10:13.

PRAYER:

Dear Lord, sometimes I doubt my own conversion. Am I truly a member of Your family? Or did I just "join the church?"

But Lord, there are some things that make me feel I must belong to You:

> the joy that rushes over me when I lift my heart in worship,
>
> the peace that is so deep inside—that no surface problem touches,
>
> the love I have for You and the love You give me for others,
>
> the relief I feel when I confess my sin and realize You have said, "Forgiven,"
>
> the comfort that comes from being able to talk to You, alone, uninterrupted,
>
> the way Your Word opens up to me when I take time to study,
>
> the real answers to my prayers.

And as I meditate on these things my soul feels satisfied.

PROMISE:

"For whosoever shall do the will of my Father which is in heaven, the same is my brother, and sister, and mother" Matt. 12:50.

"By this shall all men know that ye are my disciples, if ye have love one to another" John 13:35.

53 JOY

"Rejoice in the Lord alway: and again I say, Rejoice" Phil. 4:4.

PRAYER:

Oh, Lord, "joy" is such a tiny word, but so full of big meaning. Thank You for these big things that make my heart sing—

> the Lord Jesus Christ going to Calvary—for me,
> the victory He gives me over sin,
> the way He conquered death and took the sting out of dying,
> the fact of His resurrection,
> the knowledge that He is alive right now and at Your right hand,

and that He knows my name.

PROMISE:

"Now we rejoice in our wonderful new relationship with God—all because of what our Lord Jesus Christ has done in dying for our sins—making us friends of God" Rom. 5:11, TLB.

"I waited patiently for the Lord; and he inclined unto me, and heard my cry. He brought me up also out of an horrible pit, out of the miry clay, and set my feet upon a rock, and established my goings. And he hath put a new song in my mouth, even praise unto our God: many shall see it, and fear, and shall trust in the Lord" Ps. 40:1-3.

54 LISTENING

"May the Lord bring you into an ever deeper understanding of the love of God and of the patience that comes from Christ" II Thess. 3:5, TLB.

PRAYER:

Dear Lord, I talk too much to others, when I should be listening—to You.

And when I come to You in prayer I often do all of the asking.

Even as I speak, my mind darts here and there—inattention plagues me.

Sometimes I wait until I'm in deep trouble to pray—yet I know You want me to come to You every day.

Please, Lord, don't let me flit about like a butterfly, showing off the color of my wings—my desire is to be caught in Your net for ever.

PROMISE:

"Casting down imaginations, and every high thing that exalteth itself against the knowledge of God, and bringing into captivity every thought to the obedience of Christ" II Cor. 10:5.

"But they that wait upon the Lord shall renew their strength; they shall mount up with wings as eagles; they shall run, and not be weary; and they shall walk, and not faint" Isa. 40:31.

"Abide in me, and I in you. As the branch cannot bear fruit of itself, except it abide in the vine; no more can ye, except ye abide in me" John 15:4.

55 CLOUD NINE

"Now unto him that is able to do exceeding abundantly above all that we ask or think, . . . Unto him be glory. . ." Eph. 3:20, 21a.

PRAYER:

Father in Heaven, I am so happy! My joy is spilling over!

I pinch myself to see if I am awake.

I never dreamed that You would work it out this way.

All this time I've tried to tell You how to do it.

I planned; I schemed; I asked Your approval for my ideas. And for a while I thought You had not heard.

But You answered me far better than I could ever ask.

Now my heart is full. I thank You, Lord.

From the bottom of my heart I give You thanks.

PROMISE:

"Your Father knoweth what things ye have need of, before ye ask him" Matt. 6:8b.

"Be careful for nothing; but in every thing by prayer and supplication with thanksgiving let your requests be made known unto God" Phil. 4:6.

"In every thing give thanks: for this is the will of God in Christ Jesus concerning you" I Thess. 5:18.

56 SHUT IN WITH HIM

"The Lord is my light and my salvation; whom shall I fear? the Lord is the strength of my life; of whom shall I be afraid?" Ps. 27:1.

PRAYER:

Dear Lord, I have come
    away from the noise, the busy-ness, the hassles
    into the quiet of Your Presence
    to listen as You speak.
Teach me Your holy will
Cleanse me from my faults
Strengthen my inner self
And send me forth to serve.

In Jesus' name.

PROMISE:

"Wait on the Lord: be of good courage, and he shall strengthen thine heart: wait, I say, on the Lord" Ps. 27:14.

"And it shall come to pass, that before they call, I will answer; and while they are yet speaking, I will hear" Isa. 65:24.

"Ye have not, because ye ask not" James 4:2b.

"If ye abide in me, and my words abide in you, ye shall ask what ye will, and it shall be done unto you" John 15:7.

57 MANY QUESTIONS—ONE ANSWER

"Also I heard the voice of the Lord, saying, Whom shall I send, and who will go for us?" Isa. 6:8a.

PRAYER:

Dear Lord, I am so concerned; my heart cries out for the whole world—
little children everywhere, dying of hunger
(and I sit here well-filled)
political corruption, touching nation after nation
(where are the Christian leaders?)
thousands, with no one to care about them
(and I'm surrounded by Your love)
lost people who know nothing about Jesus
(and I have the audacity to be complacent about my salvation)

What is the answer, Lord?

PROMISE:

"Go ye therefore, and teach all nations, baptizing them in the name of the Father, and of the Son, and of the Holy Ghost" Matt. 28:19.

"Sing unto the Lord, bless his name; shew forth his salvation from day to day. Declare his glory among the heathen, his wonders among all people" Ps. 96:2, 3.

"The fruit of the righteous is a tree of life; and he that winneth souls is wise" Prov. 11:30.

"As my Father hath sent me, even so send I you" John 20:21b.

MY RESPONSE:

"Then said I, Here am I; send me" Isa. 6:8b.

58 STANDING ON THE THRESHOLD

"And remember, I am with you always, day by day, until the close of the age" Matt. 28:20b, Weymouth.

PRAYER:

Today I stand on the threshold of a New Year.

Dear Lord, I am aware that there is an equal amount of time for everyone in the year ahead.

(Help me to use that time wisely.)

And almost every young person will have the power to make the big decisions in his life.

(I may have the power, Lord, but I don't have the wisdom.)

And we still have the privilege to worship as we choose.

(I choose to worship You.)

The New Year will undoubtedly bring its problems.

(Oh, keep me close to Yourself. You are the Problem Solver.)

There are uncertainties all around us.

(But I am certain of the One who controls my life.)

Lord, help me to live out this year guided, controlled, and kept by Your love.

PROMISE:

"Let every soul be subject unto the higher powers. For there is no power but of God: the powers that be are ordained of God" Rom. 13:1.

"So teach us to number our days, that we may apply our hearts unto wisdom" Ps. 90:12.

"Only be thou strong and very courageous, that thou mayest observe to do according to all the law" Josh. 1:7a.

59 THANKSGIVING DAY

"Bless the Lord, O my soul; and all that is within me, bless his holy name" Ps. 103:1.

PRAYER:

Dear Lord, today we'll sit around and stuff ourselves with food and say "Thank You" in a very matter-of-fact way.

It seems that we take for granted everything You did for us this past year.

Seldom do we express joy for all of the food on our table, or the cars in our garage, or the nice home we live in.

We rarely praise You for the beautiful church which is the center of so much of our lives.

Lord, help us to realize that Thanksgiving Day is more than just a day to get out of school and to see who can eat the most turkey.

Thank You for providing for us so bountifully, for taking care of us so well, and for loving us so much.

PROMISE:

"Let us offer the sacrifice of praise to God continually, that is, the fruit of our lips giving thanks to his name" Heb. 13:15.

"And whatsoever ye do in word or deed, do all in the name of the Lord Jesus, giving thanks to God and the Father by him" Col. 3:17.

"Bless the Lord, O my soul, and forget not all his benefits" Ps. 103:2.

60 THE GLOW OF CHRISTMAS

"Glory to God in the highest, and on earth peace, good will toward men" Luke 2:14.

PRAYER:

Dear Lord, it's Christmas time again and my heart is filled with love. I want to say thank you—
- for the baby Jesus—who became my Savior
- for Mary—so humble and sweet, when she had so much to brag about
- for Joseph—a man who believed God in a difficult situation
- for the angel—and his announcement that has been heard around the world
- for the heavenly host—whose "Glory to God" still echoes down through time
- for the shepherds—who hurried to Him in the manger and went back to their flocks with praise in their hearts
- for the wise men—who literally fell down in worship
- for the innkeeper—who teaches us all to make room

Help me, Lord, to keep the Christmas light shining in my heart all year long.

PROMISE:

"But when the fulness of the time was come, God sent forth his Son, made of a woman, made under the law, to redeem them that were under the law" Gal. 4:4, 5a.

"For unto us a child is born, unto us a son is given: and the government shall be upon his shoulder: and his name shall be called Wonderful, Counsellor, The mighty God, The everlasting Father, The Prince of Peace" Isa. 9:6.